WITHDRAWN

STATE PROFILES

IOWA

BY NATHAN SOMMER

BLASTOFF! DISCOVERY

BELLWETHER MEDIA • MINNEAPOLIS, MN

Blastoff! Discovery launches a new mission: reading to learn. Filled with facts and features, each book offers you an exciting new world to explore!

This edition first published in 2022 by Bellwether Media, Inc.

No part of this publication may be reproduced in whole or in part without written permission of the publisher.
For information regarding permission, write to Bellwether Media, Inc., Attention: Permissions Department,
6012 Blue Circle Drive, Minnetonka, MN 55343.

Library of Congress Cataloging-in-Publication Data

Names: Sommer, Nathan, author.
Title: Iowa / by Nathan Sommer.
Description: Minneapolis, MN : Bellwether Media, Inc., 2022. |
   Series: Blastoff! Discovery: State profiles | Includes bibliographical
   references and index. | Audience: Ages 7-13 | Audience: Grades 4-6 |
   Summary: "Engaging images accompany information about Iowa.
   The combination of high-interest subject matter and narrative text is
   intended for students in grades 3 through 8"– Provided by publisher.
Identifiers: LCCN 2021019661 (print) | LCCN 2021019662 (ebook) |
   ISBN 9781644873861 (library binding) | ISBN 9781648341632 (ebook)
Subjects: LCSH: Iowa–Juvenile literature.
Classification: LCC F621.3 .S63 2022 (print) | LCC F621.3 (ebook) |
   DDC 977.7–dc23
LC record available at https://lccn.loc.gov/2021019661
LC ebook record available at https://lccn.loc.gov/2021019662

Editor: Kate Moening   Designer: Jeffrey Kollock

Printed in the United States of America, North Mankato, MN.

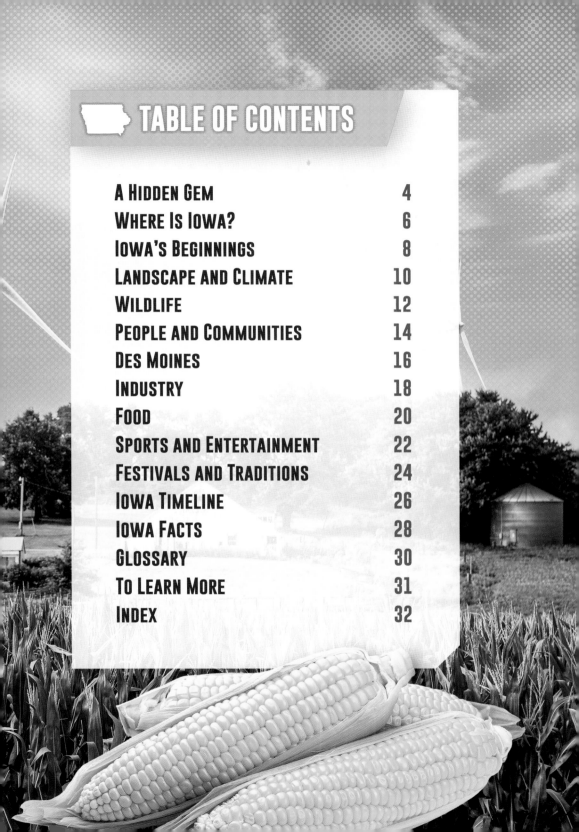

TABLE OF CONTENTS

SHRINE OF THE GROTTO OF THE REDEMPTION
WEST BEND

A family travels through the **Midwest**. Their first stop in Iowa is West Bend's **Shrine** of the **Grotto** of the **Redemption**. This giant stone shrine to Mary, the mother of Jesus, looks out of place next to the cornfields around it.

AMANA COLONIES

BRIDGES OF MADISON COUNTY

EFFIGY MOUNDS NATIONAL MONUMENT

MAQUOKETA CAVES STATE PARK

The Grotto is built from materials such as **petrified wood**, quartz, and purple amethysts. The family looks in wonder as they explore the gem-filled hallways. Many of the rock formations show scenes from the life of Jesus Christ. The journey ends at the Christmas Chapel. This colorful room features rocks from almost every country. Iowa is full of fun surprises!

Iowa sits in the center of the midwestern United States. Minnesota borders Iowa to the north. Wisconsin and Illinois lie to the east across the Mississippi River. Missouri sits to Iowa's south. Nebraska shares Iowa's western edge along the Missouri River. South Dakota completes the western border.

Des Moines, the capital city, is located in south-central Iowa. The city is named after the river that flows through it. At 56,273 square miles (145,746 square kilometers), Iowa is the 26th largest state. It is nicknamed the Hawkeye State.

SOUTH DAKOTA

● SIOUX CITY

MISSOURI RIVER

NEBRASKA

MINNESOTA

WISCONSIN

MISSISSIPPI
RIVER ———

IOWA

AMES
•

CEDAR RAPIDS
•

DES MOINES
★

IOWA CITY
•

DAVENPORT
•

ILLINOIS

MAMMOTH ZONE

Giant woolly mammoths used
to roam Iowa in large numbers.
The extinct animal's huge
bones are found underground
around the state.

MISSOURI

MESKWAKI
DANCERS

Early Native Americans came to Iowa 14,000 years ago.
They hunted large mammoths and bison. Mill Creek and
Oneota people arrived over time. They began using farming
and fishing to survive. French explorers were the first Europeans
in Iowa, arriving in 1673. They traded fur with the Sauk and
Meskwaki groups in the 1700s. They also worked with the
Meskwaki to mine lead.

The United States bought Iowa through the **Louisiana Purchase** in 1803. Early **settlers** soon arrived to farm the state's rich soil. Iowa became the 29th state on December 28th, 1846.

IOWA AND THE CIVIL WAR

Many formerly enslaved people entered Iowa through the Underground Railroad before and during the Civil War. This network of people and places offered safety to those seeking freedom.

NATIVE PEOPLES OF IOWA

MESKWAKI NATION

- Original lands in Michigan and eastern Wisconsin, then eastern Iowa after the Fox Wars
- About 800 on the Meskwaki Nation settlement
- Also called Sac & Fox Tribe of the Mississippi, Sac (Sauk), and Fox (Meskwaki)

OMAHA

- Original lands in Ohio, followed by northern Missouri, northwestern Iowa, and eastern Nebraska
- 2,500 to 3,000 on the Omaha Reservation (most in Nebraska)

WINNEBAGO

- Original lands in central Wisconsin and northern Illinois, then northeastern Iowa
- About 2,600 on the Winnebago Reservation (most in Nebraska)
- Also called Ho-Chunk

9

Iowa is mostly **plains**. Much of the state is used for farmland, especially in flat northern and central Iowa. Lakes also dot the land there. Large, steep hills and cliffs cover northeastern Iowa's Driftless Area. The south is filled with rolling hills and grasslands. Most of the state's streams and rivers empty into the Mississippi River in the east.

MISSISSIPPI RIVER —

DRIFTLESS AREA

PIKES PEAK STATE PARK
MISSISSIPPI RIVER

IOWA'S CHALLENGE: FLOODING

Climate change is making Iowa's floods even worse. The increase in flooding makes it harder for farmers to grow crops. It also damages buildings and homes.

SEASONAL HIGHS AND LOWS

SPRING
HIGH: 59°F (15°C)
LOW: 38°F (3°C)

SUMMER
HIGH: 83°F (28°C)
LOW: 61°F (16°C)

FALL
HIGH: 61°F (16°C)
LOW: 40°F (4°C)

WINTER
HIGH: 31°F (-1°C)
LOW: 13°F (-11°C)

°F = degrees Fahrenheit
°C = degrees Celsius

Iowa experiences all four seasons. Heavy rainfall paired with melting snow creates heavy floods in the spring. The state's flat lands often face tornadoes during the hot summer months. Some tornadoes are strong enough to throw cars!

OPOSSUMS

Iowa has few homes for animals today. Farms and cities took over much of the **tallgrass prairie** that once covered the state. But deer, opossums, and raccoons still make homes in Iowa. They protect their young from hungry coyotes and bobcats.

BOBCAT

Iowa is also home to hundreds of birds. Goldfinches visit feeders in backyards. Ring-necked pheasants eat insects, seeds, and crops in the state's farmland. Peregrine falcons dive for prey from great heights. During Iowa winters, bald eagles fly near lakes and rivers. Ospreys pluck bass and trout out of the water!

RING-NECKED PHEASANTS

WHITE-TAILED DEER

OSPREY

AMERICAN GOLDFINCH

Life Span: up to 11 years
Status: least concern

American goldfinch range =

LEAST CONCERN	NEAR THREATENED	VULNERABLE	ENDANGERED	CRITICALLY ENDANGERED	EXTINCT IN THE WILD	EXTINCT

13

Iowa is home to more than 3.1 million people. Over half live in or near cities. The Des Moines area is home to nearly 700,000 people. In general, Iowa's population is growing older. Many younger Iowans live near universities in Ames and Iowa City.

HOG WILD

Hogs outnumber humans by about 20 million in Iowa! The state is the leading pork producer in the United States.

AMES

IOWA STATE UNIVERSITY

STATE

SUKUP END ZONE CLUB

REIMAN PLAZA

FAMOUS IOWAN

Name: Harrison Barnes

Born: May 30, 1992

Hometown: Ames, Iowa

Famous For: Basketball forward in the NBA who has played with the Golden State Warriors, Dallas Mavericks, and Sacramento Kings and won an NBA championship with the Warriors

About 9 out of every 10 Iowans are white. Most of them have German, British, and Dutch backgrounds. A growing number of Hispanic Americans are moving to Iowa. Most have Mexican backgrounds. Smaller numbers of Asian Americans and African or Black Americans also continue to grow. Very few Native Americans remain in Iowa.

Des Moines was first built as a **fort** in 1843 to protect the Sauk and Meskwaki people. But white settlers forced these groups to leave in 1845. Des Moines became Iowa's capital in 1857.
The city grew quickly after coal was discovered nearby in the early 1900s.

THE GOLDEN DOME

The dome atop Iowa's State Capitol is one of the largest in the United States. A layer of gold leaf makes it shine!

PAPPAJOHN SCULPTURE PARK

Cheap living and an educated population make Des Moines a top city for business. Art lovers enjoy the Des Moines Art Center and Pappajohn Sculpture Park. Downtown, the Principal Riverwalk connects Iowans to more than 80 miles (129 kilometers) of walking and bike trails.

WIND ENERGY

Farming has always been important to Iowa's economy. Rich soil makes it a perfect place to grow many crops. The state is a leader in corn, soybean, and livestock production. Wind energy is a growing power source and job creator. Nearly half of Iowa's electricity comes from wind!

Most Iowans today have **service jobs**. Many work for banks and **insurance** companies. Des Moines is considered a world leader in insurance. It is also a growing center for technology. Facebook and Microsoft have built **data centers** nearby.

IOWA'S FUTURE: TEACHERS NEEDED

Fewer Iowans are choosing to become teachers. This has led to a shortage, especially in special education and small town schools. Iowa will need to find creative ways to teach all students and to encourage more people to become teachers.

INVENTED IN IOWA

ICE CREAM BARS
Date Invented: 1922
Inventor: Christian Nelson

BREAD SLICER
Date Invented: 1928
Inventor: Otto Frederick Rohwedder

THE BUTTERFLY STROKE
Date Invented: 1934 (disputed)
Inventor: David Armbruster

TRAMPOLINE
Date Invented: 1930s
Inventors: George Nissen and Larry Griswald

19

BREADED PORK
TENDERLOIN

Iowans love their local food. With so much farmland, they have many options! Breaded pork tenderloins are a favorite at many restaurants. These are eaten solo or as a sandwich. Loose meat sandwiches also frequent menus. Iowans know these as Maid-Rites!

EGG-CELLENT PRODUCTION

No state produces more eggs than Iowa. Its hens laid more than 16 billion eggs in 2019! That is nearly one out of every five eggs in the United States!

Many say Iowa sweet corn is the best in the world. It is hard to imagine a summer festival or fair without the state's famous corn on the cob. Morel mushroom hunting is popular in Iowa's woodlands. Iowans cook these with butter or enjoy them deep-fried!

MAID-RITE SANDWICH

MOREL MUSHROOMS

STOVETOP CORN ON THE COB

Have an adult help you cook up some of Iowa's famous corn!

INGREDIENTS

6 ears yellow sweet corn, shucked
butter
salt

6 SERVINGS

DIRECTIONS

1. Fill a large pot about 3/4 full of water and bring to a boil.

2. Gently place the ears of corn into the boiling water, cover the pot, and turn off the heat.

3. Let the corn cook in the hot water until tender, about 10 minutes.

4. Drain the water.

5. Season your corn with butter and salt and enjoy!

Iowans get outside in all four seasons. In fall, many people hunt white-tailed deer in the state's grasslands. Winter brings ice fishers to Big Creek State Park. In warmer months, Iowans often hike in state parks. They travel through caves, tallgrass prairies, and woodlands.

BIXBY STATE PRESERVE

FIELD OF DREAMS

The popular baseball movie *Field of Dreams* was filmed in Dyersville, Iowa. Released in 1989, its filming site still draws thousands of visitors each year!

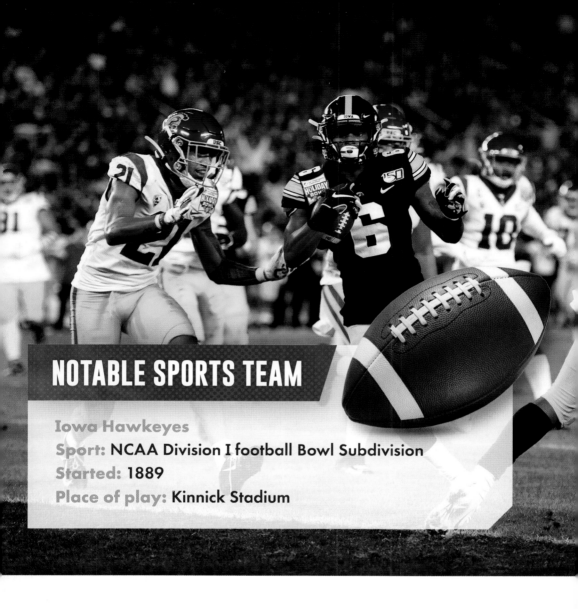

NOTABLE SPORTS TEAM

Iowa Hawkeyes
Sport: NCAA Division I football Bowl Subdivision
Started: 1889
Place of play: Kinnick Stadium

College football rules Iowa in the fall. Iowans love to watch the University of Iowa and Iowa State teams face off each year. Many Iowans also take in fall colors along the Des Moines River or visit the Des Moines **Botanical Garden**.

The Iowa State Fair in August is Iowa's largest party. More than one million people attend to go on rides and see award-winning livestock. The fair also features more than 80 foods on a stick! Many Iowans celebrate their German **heritage** at Maifest each May. Thousands visit the Amana **Colonies** for the Maifest parade and **traditional** German dances.

Iowa is the first state to **caucus** in each presidential election. This means Iowans have the first say in deciding the next president. Iowans are proud of their midwestern roots. They celebrate the hard work that keeps their state going!

THE WORLD–FAMOUS BUTTER COW

The Butter Cow is the star of the Iowa State Fair. Each year, around 600 pounds (272 kilograms) of butter are used to make it!

IOWA STATE FAIR
DES MOINES

BLUE
LINE
PARKING
SHUTTLE

25

1843

Fort Des Moines is built to protect the Sauk and Meskwaki Native Americans, but the groups are later forced out of Iowa

1673

French explorers Louis Jolliet and Jacques Marquette explore what is now Iowa, and France soon claims ownership

1820

The Missouri Compromise ensures Iowa will be a non-slave state

1803

The United States buys Iowa as a part of the Louisiana Purchase

1846

Iowa becomes the 29th state

1854

The first Iowa State Fair is held

2020

Iowa is hit hard with strong winds, thunderstorms, and tornadoes in an event called the August Midwest derecho

1922

May Francis becomes the first woman to be elected to a state-wide leadership position in Iowa

1917

Fort Des Moines becomes the first training center for Black troops during World War I

1993

Major flooding causes billions of dollars in damage throughout the state

Nicknames: The Hawkeye State, The Corn State

Motto: "Our liberties we prize and our rights we will maintain."

Date of Statehood: December 28, 1846 (the 29th state)

Capital City: Des Moines ★

Other Major Cities: Cedar Rapids, Davenport, Sioux City, Iowa City, Ames

Area: 56,273 square miles (145,746 square kilometers); Iowa is the 26th largest state.

Population

3,190,369
(2020)

STATE FLAG

The Iowa flag has three vertical stripes of red, white, and blue. The blue stands for justice, the white represents purity, and the red stands for courage. In the middle is a bald eagle carrying the state's motto.

INDUSTRY

Main Exports

soybeans

corn

pork

machinery

JOBS

MANUFACTURING
11%

FARMING AND
NATURAL
RESOURCES
5%

GOVERNMENT
13%

SERVICES
71%

Natural Resources
soil, coal, gypsum, limestone

GOVERNMENT

Federal Government

4 REPRESENTATIVES | 2 SENATORS

6 ELECTORAL VOTES

USA

IA

State Government

100 REPRESENTATIVES | 50 SENATORS

STATE SYMBOLS

STATE BIRD
AMERICAN GOLDFINCH

STATE ROCK
GEODE

STATE FLOWER
WILD PRAIRIE ROSE

STATE TREE
OAK

botanical garden—a large, usually public garden where plants are grown in order to be studied

caucus—to meet with other people of the same political party in order to vote for the party's next leader

colonies—groups of people with common characteristics or interests that live close to one another

data centers—buildings that house large computer networks; companies use data centers to store huge amounts of information.

fort—a strong building where soldiers live

grotto—a cave or a structure built to look like a cave

heritage—the traditions, achievements, and beliefs that are part of the history of a group of people

insurance—a business in which people pay money for protection against injuries or damages

Louisiana Purchase—a deal made between France and the United States; it gave the United States 828,000 square miles (2,144,510 square kilometers) of land west of the Mississippi River.

Midwest—a region of 12 states in the north-central United States

petrified wood—plant fossils that form when plants are buried and minerals replace the plant material over time

plains—large areas of flat land

redemption—the act of making a bad or unpleasant thing better

service jobs—jobs that perform tasks for people or businesses

settlers—people who move to live in a new, undeveloped region

shrine—a place where people often go to worship that is connected with a holy person or event

tallgrass prairie—a wide area of flat land where many types of tall grasses grow

traditional—related to customs, ideas, or beliefs handed down from one generation to the next

AT THE LIBRARY

Arnéz, Lynda. *Native Peoples of the Great Plains.*
New York, N.Y.: Gareth Stevens Publishing, 2017.

Haynes, Danielle. *Presidential Primaries and Caucuses.* New York, N.Y.: Powerkids Press, 2020.

Lowe, Alexander. *Iowa Hawkeyes.* New York, N.Y.: AV2 by Weigel, 2020.

ON THE WEB

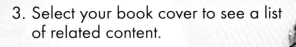

FACTSURFER

Factsurfer.com gives you a safe, fun way to find more information.

1. Go to www.factsurfer.com.

2. Enter "Iowa" into the search box and click 🔍.

3. Select your book cover to see a list of related content.

INDEX